THE BATTLE OF ALGIERS

Algeria's Fight for Independence

Written by Xavier De Weirt
In collaboration with Mathieu Beaud
Translated by Carly Probert

History 50MINUTES.com

THE BATTLE OF ALGIERS

KEY INFORMATION

- **When:** 7 January – 8 October 1957
- **Where:** Algiers
- **Context:** The Algerian War (1954-1962)
- **Belligerents:** France against the Algerian National Liberation Front (FLN)
- **Commanders and leaders:**
  - Jacques Massu, French General (1908-2002)
  - Roger Trinquier, French superior paratrooper officer (1908-1986)
  - Mohamed Larbi Ben M'hidi, responsible for armed action in Algiers (1923-1957)
  - Yacef Saâdi, head of the autonomous zone of Algiers (born in 1928)
- **Outcome:** French victory
- **Victims:**
  - Algerian camp: between 1 000 and 3 000 deaths
  - French camp: approximately 374 dead and 917 wounded

INTRODUCTION

The Battle of Algiers, also called the "great repression", was a particularly painful episode in the Algerian war, which was rooted in the context of decolonization. The fighting lasted for nine months between the 10th Parachute Division of General Jacques Massu and the Algerian nationalist National Liberation Front (FLN). Unlike a conventional war between two armies, it was, on the part of France, a true commando operation, whose methods would later be denounced by international public opinion.

In the summer of 1956, the center of Algiers was shaken by a series of terrorist attacks by the FLN which, wanting to destabilize French society and demonstrate to the world the legitimacy of its fight for independence, aimed for the center of French power in Algeria. Directly threatened, France decided to fight back and on 7 January 1957, the troops of General Jacques Massu entered the kasbah of Algiers, a Muslim neighborhood where nearly 75 000 individuals resided. There, the French soldiers defended themselves by leading a war against insurgency, using techniques that were developed by studying the Viet Minh (Vietnamese political and paramilitary organization) during the Indochina War (1946-1954).

While the deadly bombings of the FLN multiplied, thus radicalizing the French population in Algeria even more, French paratroopers and commandos identified, searched, questioned, imprisoned, tortured and killed in order to dismantle the terrorist resistance network. The battle ended in October 1957 with the arrest of the most influential members, marking the dismantling of the FLN, and temporarily ending the violence. Although the Battle of Algiers was only a short episode of the conflict, it would serve to denounce the abuses committed by France in its struggle to keep Algeria French. Indeed, cornered by critics, the government decided, under the authority of Charles de Gaulle (1890-1970), to abandon the fighting and, on 18 March 1962,

France signed the Evian agreements to enshrine the independence of Algeria after eight years of fierce resistance.

POLITICAL AND SOCIAL CONTEXT

THE DECOLONIZATION PHENOMENON

In the 19th century, colonization was carried out by a handful of European countries, including Britain, France, the Netherlands, Belgium, Germany and Italy, which possessed all of Africa and much of Asia by the end of the century, therefore ruling over hundreds of millions of people. The two world wars (1914-1918 and 1939-1945), however, marked the cessation of European settlement. The prestige of France and Britain was indeed heavily marred by numerous military defeats and the significance of human and material losses suffered during the fighting.

Moreover, the people of Europe were gradually becoming aware of the dire living conditions of the colonized peoples, while, from the interwar period, independence movements were emerging in the colonies, led by a few intellectual elite. These movements more or less succeeded in rallying the masses which remained largely illiterate. During the Second World War, due to the weakened colonial control and the forced recruitment of thousands of colonial fighters, these movements were radicalized and emitted claims in order to obtain their emancipation. In the Middle East, some colonies took advantage of this change in the balance of power to claim their independence. This was particularly the case with Syria and Lebanon, who gained independence from France in September 1941 and November 1943 respectively.

Although in 1945, France and Britain still occupied most of

the colonized space, they had lost a significant part of their economic power and prestige. That is why France, defeated by the German army in 1940, was keen to retain its empire, while Britain, undefeated and more pragmatic, considered the situation more in terms of economic interest.

The United Nations Charter signed in 1945 marked the birth of the UN and also proclaimed the right of all peoples to be self-determined, which would be interpreted by the colonies as a call to intensify the claims.

While some colonies gained independence in a relatively calm manner, often in exchange for territorial or political economic benefits, others were forced to resort to arms in order to achieve this ideal. However, after the weakening of the European nations during the Second World War, the tension from the Cold War (1947-1989) facilitated the process of decolonization.

GOOD TO KNOW

The Cold War was an ideological conflict fought between 1947 and 1989, with a Western bloc led by the United States against an Eastern bloc led by the Soviet Union. The term "cold" refers to the fact that, during this period, there would never be a direct armed conflict between the two main belligerents.

While the Americans and the Russians were the big winners of the Second World War, they strongly opposed the colonial aspirations of the European powers. The first, having achieved independence from Britain in

1776, had defended the freedom of peoples to choose their own form of government ever since. The Soviets in turn followed the precepts of the founding father Vladimir Illyich Lenin (1870-1924), who advocated the emancipation of the peoples on the way to the revolution. However, the ideological divide between the two powers affected the demands for independence of the colonized peoples. This was very visible in Asia, where a Russian-Chinese mainland influenced by communism opposed a Southern Asia that opened on seas under American influence. Since then, several leaders of independence movements who had openly proclaimed themselves Marxists (movement of thought advocating class warfare) had been at the head of influential communist parties. Meanwhile, the United States maintained colonial authority in the countries remote from Marxism to ensure the cohesion of the block.

In 1955, the Bandung Conference (Indonesia) was held, bringing together the leaders of the former colonies, led by Gamal Abdel Nasser, the future Egyptian president (1918-1970). They were aiming to stand out from the bipolar logic of the Cold War (anti-imperialism versus anti-communism) by becoming champions of anti-colonialism. This movement born of the Cold War logically amplified the liberation movements for independence, particularly in Africa.

The Philippines, one of the few American colonies, was the first to achieve independence after the war. This was followed by the former British colonies of India, Pakistan,

Burma and Ceylon (Sri Lanka) in 1947. Meanwhile, France liberated the French Indochina in 1954, after eight years of war. In North Africa, Morocco and Tunisia, a French protectorate, became independent in 1956. The majority of the sub-Saharan French and British African colonies would be released between 1957 and 1962.

The French defeat at Dien Bien Phu on 7 May 1954 marked the end of the Indochina war and the opening of negotiations for Vietnam's independence. The conflict lasted for eight years (1946-1954), fought between the French armed forces and the troops of communist leader Ho Chi Minh (Vietnamese statesman, 1890-1969). The latter indeed benefitted from the colonial weakening during the war to establish a Republic of Vietnam in northern Indochina. Ho Chi Minh therefore tried to convince the French to withdraw and recognize the Vietnamese Republic, but maintain political and economic influence in the country. The French refused and bombarded Haiphong (strategic port), triggering the war. The conflict would later fit into the logic of the Cold War, with the Russians supporting North Vietnam and Ho Chi Minh and the United States supporting the French troops in the south. But, ill-prepared for a *maquis* war (guerrilla warfare), the French were eventually trapped and surrounded by an army, mainly made up of civilians.

Vietnam was recognized as an independent state by

the Geneva Accords of 21 July 1954. This huge humiliation for France would encourage France even further to maintain what remained of its colonial empire. Furthermore, the observation of Indochinese combat methods would be of great use for the repression of Algeria that began a few days later.

In a tense international atmosphere, the Russians and Americans supported the cause of the oppressed people against the colonial powers and signed various pacts of alliance in order to garner as many people as possible to their cause. The whole world was affected by this phenomenon:

- In Asia, anti-colonial movements took a considerably Marxist character, particularly due to the proximity of Russian and Chinese examples;
- Black African independence movements took off, with a slight delay, and were also supported by the Marxists;
- In North Africa, nationalism would be strongly pushed by the birth of the Arab sense of identity, embodied by the Egyptian Gamal Abdel Nasser.

THE COLONIAL SYSTEM IN ALGERIA

The French colonization of Algeria in 1830 was particularly violent. On 5 July 1830, French troops seized Algiers and took control of a territory that they had been coveting for years, ending the Turkish occupation exercised since the 16th century. Much of the territory was bloodily conquered over 17 years. Algeria was proclaimed French territory on

12 November 1848. Due to its proximity to the metropolis, the country was to serve as a settler colony for France. This undermined Algerian culture by imposing the religion, language and an economic system. In the 1850s and 1860s, many French, but also Southern Europeans, Germans and Swiss then crossed the Mediterranean with the aim of settling on these fallow lands. The territory was divided and distributed to the great disadvantage of the local people, who were pushed into the southern desert and the mountains while the newcomers seized huge arable land plots. In order to establish the French character of the territory, the colonial authorities implemented a very unequal assimilation policy from 1870, which bordered on racism, offering full French citizenship first to the Jews, then to the Europeans of Algeria (1889). The Arab population obtained only a secondary status in the judicial context of the Code of Indigenous Status, an administrative system that was introduced for all populations colonized by the French Empire in 1881.

With the French "pacification" of 1848, a particularly difficult political and economic system was thus established for the Algerian population, which held French nationality without the benefit of citizenship, making them a second-class population. Discrimination was visible at all levels of society, particularly within education since the local people had almost no access to schooling. Only a small minority of Algerians from the middle class gained access to adequate education, but this was still very limited compared to that provided to the French. On the other hand, the Aboriginal population was also subject to economic discrimination.

Arab families living in the city were thus pushed to the outskirts. The French system destroyed the Algerian farmer and commercial structures by taking approximately 3 million hectares of fertile land from the farmers and 3.5 million hectares of forested area for its own benefit. To maintain their agrarian activities, the farmers were forced to flee to the countryside and desert areas, to migrate to the outskirts of the Europeanized cities, or to work on the farms of the Algerian Frenchmen. The situation had barely settled when the economic crisis of the thirties struck, which accentuated the rural exodus of local populations and led to the creation of the first shantytowns in major urban centers such as Algiers and Constantine (city of north-eastern Algeria). These massive movements led to the impoverishment of cities which were now predominantly European and gave rise to serious social tensions.

It was in this context that the first independence movements emerged. However, these came from Algerian scholars from the middle class and the large rural families, and remained rather isolated in their action as the French administration had deliberately excluded 95% of Muslims from education.

These movements were divided into three main branches, which were as follows:

- A progressive and democratic current led by Ferhat Abbas (Algerian politician, 1899-1985);
- A traditionalist current turned to Islam, led by the *ulama* (doctors of Islamic law, jurists and theologians);
- A revolutionary nationalist movement founded by Ahmed Hadj Messali (Algerian nationalist, 1899-1974).

These movements were strengthened during the Second World War. In 1942, the American landing in North Africa raised great hopes for the Algerians who were waiting for recognition from France, which had largely used them to fight against Germany. But, on 8 May 1945, when the Germans surrendered, insurrection broke out during a demonstration in the town of Setif of Algeria in order to claim the country's independence, to which France replied with fierce repression, causing thousands of deaths.

THE NATIONAL LIBERATION FRONT

The National Liberation Front was founded on 10 October 1954 in Cairo by nine historic leaders, originally from the Algerian People's Party (PPA). The PPA was a nationalist independence movement founded by Ahmed Hadj Messali in 1937, which would later take the name of the Movement for the Triumph of Democratic Liberties (BACT) in 1946.

In 1945, the massacres in Setif revived the seed of an activist trend in the Algerian People's Party. Two years later, its most vocal advocates worked within the Special Organization, which quickly became the armed wing of the party and the MTLD. These activists were young Algerians from mostly rural old noble classes, whose parents had been stripped of their power. Supporters of the armed struggle, they increasingly opposed the legalistic and conciliatory natures of other movements, including those of their charismatic leader Ahmed Hadj Messali. Shortly after the opening of hostilities by the National Liberation Front in what would later become the Algerian war, the latter founded the

Algerian National Movement, which remained one of the few political opponents of the FLN, provoking fratricidal violence between both camps.

The leadership of the National Liberation Front was composed of six members from the inside, spread in different regions of the colony (*wilayas*). It was they who directed and instigated the fighting, while three external members were stationed in Cairo, where they maintained relations with various Arab resistance movements and took care of the supply of weapons. Alongside, the FLN sought to unify the Algerian resistance movement by merging various separatists trends, which occurred at the Congress of Soummam held on 20 August 1956. Together, they specified the internal organization, as well as military objectives for the political project of the Front for Algeria. At the top was the National Council of the Algerian Revolution (CNRA), a collegiate body which took fundamental decisions, as well as the coordination and implementation committee (CEC) which was responsible for the proper implementation thereof. Becoming a true single party, the FLN was gradually positioning itself as the exclusive representative of all Algerians.

It also had its own fighters within the National Liberation Army. This battalion trained men especially for the guerrilla warfare, the *mujahideen*, who led the guerrillas in rural areas, as well as unarmed collaborators who were in charge of supplies, stewardship and surveillance. At the height of the war in Algeria in 1956 and 1958, the army had about 20 000 *mujahideen* and many unarmed auxiliaries.

THE START OF THE WAR IN ALGERIA

When the war broke out in Algeria on 1 November 1954, only a few fighters were actually involved and the population had not yet joined the fight of the FLN. However, several attacks and acts of sabotage were held in different regions of the country in order to undermine the opponent. As for the French, they were trying to maintain order through a vast military and police force, mass arming and strong repression. Moreover, on 31 March 1955, the government of Edgar Faure (French politician, 1908-1988) expanded the powers of the French army for the first time and introduced hosting camps that aimed to stop suspects from participating in these rebellions and to dismantle the networks. Denounced by some opponents as genuine concentration camps, they served as a base to neutralize and interrogate without reason any individuals who were considered dangerous.

With the Bandung Conference, the FLN succeeded in their fight to be heard by the UN, causing an internationalization of the conflict that would prove crucial to the outcome of the war. Battles took place mainly in rural and desert areas of the territory (the *djebels*), where fighters of the NLA, to counter the French repression, practiced guerrilla tactics, harassment and sabotage, while making full use of propaganda aimed at villagers to encourage them to join their project.

However, the war took a different form after the terrorist attack of Constantine on 20 and 21 August 1955. In a poor region where the coexistence of European and Muslim communities was particularly tense, the regional leader Youssef Zighout (1921-1956) managed to raise an insurrection that led to the killing of many French people, in order to elicit reactions and publicize their actions. Feeling its honor had been attacked, France took on 60 000 young reservists and decided to severely punish the attack. From then on, new soldiers were regularly sent to Algeria. While in January, the French army only had about 70 000 soldiers, the number rose to 170 000 men in December. These figures continued to grow after this and on the eve of the Battle of Algiers, the French army had no less than 350 000 men, the majority of whom were barely 20 years old. By 1958, the number of soldiers exceeded 400 000 individuals.

On 2 January 1956, a new left-wing government was formed in France, headed by the socialist Prime Minister Guy Mollet (1905-1975). After receiving a very hostile reception from the French during his first trip to Algeria, the politician, who had been rather moderated until then, decided to restore order in the colony. To do this, he obtained the special powers of the National Assembly, which enabled him to take all necessary measures for the restoration of order, the protection of life and property, as well as the safeguarding of the territory. In March 1956, he appointed Robert Lacoste (1898-1989) as governor of Algeria to further strengthen repression. These measures were unpopular among the Algerians and provoked new clashes, following which acts of violence occurred more and more regularly. The FLN launched a wave of deadly attacks and ambushes which directly intended to trap the young French soldiers who were still poorly trained on the field.

Different illegal French factions appeared here and there to respond to the FLN attacks with terrorist actions, including planting bombs, committing murders and creating private torture centers. Among these was the Organization of the French Algerian Resistance (ORAF), a network that brought together the ultras of French Algeria who made use of unconventional fighting methods. Moreover, besides the daily police and military repression, Algerian Muslims were often the target of punitive expeditions by French civilians, in retaliation of the actions of the FLN. On 10 August 1956, these French radicals carried out a deadly attack on Thebes street in the heart of the Muslim quarter of Algiers, which killed between 15 and 60 Algerian people. In France, Algerian immigrants, indirect victims of the conflict, were also subject to harsh exactions. The culmination came in the violent repression of immigrant protesters in October 1961 and on 8 February 1962 at the Charonne metro station in Paris.

THE THREAT TO ALGIERS

While mainly operating in rural areas from the beginning of the war, the FLN decided to concentrate its operations in the capital and expand its network of influence. The creation of an autonomous zone in Algiers (ZAA) was decided at the Congress of Soummam on 20 August 1956 and Yacef Saâdi was appointed as its leader to conduct urban warfare. The coordination and implementation committee, the decision-making body of the FLN, decided to settle in the kasbah of Algiers, as close as possible to the colonial power. Since the announcement of the French that party members would be executed, the FLN abandoned its plan for reactive violence, multiplied the number of attacks on Algiers and radicalized combat tactics, as well as its political message.

In mid-afternoon on 30 September, a bomb exploded at the Milk Bar and the Cafeteria, two crowded Algerian cafes. This event created true hysteria among the French population of Algeria. The attack, which killed 4 people and injured 52, was quickly claimed by the FLN. As of that date, the attacks would increase in both camps.

In December 1956, 122 attacks were orchestrated by Yacef Saâdi in the Algiers conurbation and on 27 December, Amédée Froger (1882-1956), a spokesman for the reactionary colonists, was assassinated. This event was the trigger of the Battle of Algiers and would encourage the French colonists to revolt.

COMMANDERS AND LEADERS

JACQUES MASSU, FRENCH GENERAL

Born in 1908 in a military environment, Jacques Massu was admitted to Saint-Cyr (an officer training school) in 1928 and completed his studies with the rank of lieutenant. He then entered the colonial infantry and was responsible for a Senegalese infantry regiment, before serving in Morocco and Chad (1931-1940). In June 1940, he joined the Free France (resistance organization) behind General Charles de Gaulle and worked in North Africa under the command of Colonel Philippe Leclerc de Hauteclocque (1902-1947). He was the author of several important feats of arms during the liberation of the French territory.

At the end of the war, he was sent to Indochina with the lieutenant-colonel to repel the Japanese forces and, in 1946, he took part in the war in Indochina. A patented paratrooper in 1947, he became commander of the 1st paratrooper commando half-brigade unit that he formed himself. Two years later, he was an auditor at the Institute for Advanced Studies of National Defense in Paris. It was probably during this time that he studied the techniques of psychological warfare and defense that would later be applied during the Battle of Algiers.

He was promoted to brigadier general in 1955 and took command of the intervention group of paratroopers in North Africa. He was then appointed head of the 10th paratrooper division during the Franco-British intervention in the Suez Canal crisis (October-November 1956). Having just returned from Egypt, he was called to restore order in the Battle of Algiers in January 1957. During this mission, benefitting from full police powers, he was responsible for orchestrating a ruthless repression that would put an end to the FLN, conducted in late September 1957. He was then given command of the Algerian army corps in 1958 and left the territory in 1960. In 1966, he received the rank of army general.

Until the end of his career, he worked in the supervision of the military youth and wrote several books in order to talk about his memories. He died in 2002.

ROGER TRINQUIER, FRENCH SUPERIOR PARATROOPER OFFICER

Born in 1908, superior paratrooper officer Roger Trinquier took part in the Indochina War (1946-1954), the crisis of the Suez Canal and the war in Algeria. He was a theorist of war against insurgency and a follower of the theory of parallel hierarchies by Charles Lacheroy (1906-2005), whose methodology would be the focus of French military operations during the Battle of Algiers. It was he who implemented the principles of modern warfare to counter the attacks of the FLN and uncover its networks during the Battle of Algiers.

GOOD TO KNOW

The theory of parallel hierarchies was one of the tactics of the revolutionary war. It comes from the observation of the practices of the Vietminh by Colonel Charles Lacheroy during the Indochina war and stresses the crucial importance of the rear (civilians) in the combat system and, therefore, the strategic contribution of their framework.

The control of the population stems from the articulation of two hierarchical and parallel dimensions. The first dimension is related to the territory and the positions of individuals in a space (home, neighborhood, town, etc.), while the other is related to their activity.

According to Roger Trinquier, an essential feature of subversive warfare is the fact that its scope goes beyond the armed confrontation and extends into the political, social, economic and psychological fields. He was one of the first French people to have understood what was at stake in this kind of conflict with the training of people by an underground organization, which he saw as perfectly characterizing the practices of the FLN that they needed to eradicate.

Parade of the 10th parachute division of General Jacques Massu, summer 1957.

In January 1957, he commanded a regiment of the 10th parachute division of General Jacques Massu and developed a device of urban protection, an instrument for ensuring the defense and training of people, which would be at the heart of French success in this battle. He planned to divide each block of houses in perimeters in Algiers and to appoint a French leader to each of them. Moreover, on 23rd October 1957, he set up the anti-terrorism force in the kasbah, with the objective of preventing a return of the FLN rebels in the area, whilst providing a tool for mobilization and propaganda. A campaign of identifying and registering the population, house by house, began, along with an imposed curfew, systematic raids and a right of perquisition. It was the thinking of Roger Trinquier which prompted harsh interrogations and the systematic torture of those who resisted. Indeed, his definition of terrorism meant that all soldiers engaged in the war knew of the risk they took if captured in advance and asserted that they must accept suffering and death (Trinquier 2000). In this regard, the system also planned special support missions of death squads led by General Paul Aussaresses (1918-2013), to conduct interrogations. In this context, the use of torture as a means to obtain a confession was designed to terrorize the population as well as make it adhere to the French political project.

Following the success of the Battle of Algiers, Roger Trinquier continued his activities on Algerian territory, despite the return to power of General de Gaulle, who disapproved of these revolutionary war methods. Finally sent away from the colony in 1961, he sailed to the Belgian Congo with the mission to train the police of the secessionist leader of Katanga, Moïse Tshombe (1919-1969). After its independence, he spent the rest of his life close to French Algeria and wrote several books, including an autobiography. He died in 1986.

MOHAMED LARBI BEN M'HIDI, RESPONSIBLE FOR ARMED ACTION IN ALGIERS

Born in 1923 into a marabou family, Mohamed Larbi Ben M'hidi joined separatist and nationalist circles at a young age. At the age of 17, he joined the Algerian People's Party of Messali Hadj Ahmed, then the Movement for the Triumph of Democratic Liberties, and in 1947, he became part of the Special Organization (military sector). In 1952, he became the political-military head of Oran (socio-cultural region located in western Algeria) and in April 1954, he participated in the formation of the FLN in the Revolutionary Committee of Unity and Action (CRUA). At the Congress of Soummam, he was one of the masterminds of the autonomous zone of Algiers, which would ensure the supremacy of the FLN in the center of the Algerian government. In the first weeks of the Battle of Algiers, he participated in the setting up of several attacks, in cooperation with Yacef Saâdi, of whom he was a superior. He was arrested by paratroopers in the kasbah of Algiers on 25 February 1957. Interrogated and tortured, he was taken to a farm at night by the troops of Commander Paul Aussaresses, where he was hanged. Until 2001 and the public confession of Paul Aussaresses, the death of Mohamed Larbi Ben M'hidi was officially attributed to suicide. Since then he has been considered a martyr by many Algerians.

YACEF SAÂDI, HEAD OF THE AUTONOMOUS ZONE OF ALGIERS

Yacef Saâdi was born in 1928 in Kabylia (northern Algeria), then emigrated to the kasbah of Algiers to work as a baker. In 1945, he joined the Algerian People's Party and, one year later, he became an activist in the military wing of the Movement for the Triumph of Democratic Liberties.

After a stay in France, he returned to Algeria in 1954 and joined the FLN. Arrested by the French intelligence services, he managed to deceive their vigilance and went underground. Two years later, he was elected by the FLN to mount a terrorist network that would be ready to go into action at any moment. Accompanied by Mohamed Larbi Ben M'hidi, he created the autonomous zone of Algiers and set up the "Bomb" network, which dealt with the conceptualization, realization, storage and distribution of the arsenal of war. To that end, he enlisted scientists who he turned into chemists, activists and laborers in Muslim neighborhoods. Thus, from 1956, the FLN was supplied with explosives from Morocco. Once the arsenal was produced, bombs were placed in crowded places in Algiers (bars, hotels, restaurants, etc.) by young European-looking women. Yacef Saâdi was also responsible for setting up the FLN in Algiers, which required fighting the competitors, namely the Messalists (supporters of the Algerian national movement, opposed to the FLN) of Messali Hadj Ahmed.

Dismantling of the " Bomb" network in June 1957.

On 24 September 1957, Yacef Saâdi was arrested by French paratroopers. Imprisoned and sentenced to death, his sentence was commuted on the return to power of Charles de Gaulle. He was released from jail during the Liberation in 1962. The following year, he was appointed president of the National Association of Friendship with the People by the Algerian President Ahmed Ben Bella (1916-2012). It was also during this time that he started producing films and founded Casbah Film. Notably, he produced *The Battle of Algiers*, directed by Gillo Pontecorvo. Although well-received by some as it was considered representative of the reality of the events, it was severely criticized by others, particularly due to the role played by Yacef Saâdi, who played himself. In 2001, he was appointed senator by Algerian President Abdelaziz Bouteflika (1937). Now in his late 80s, Yacef

Saâdi's activities before and after the independence have been questioned.

ANALYSIS OF THE BATTLE

METHODS OF COMBAT

The Battle of Algiers, which began in January 1957, was a particularly violent episode of the Algerian War. More than just a battle, it was a very fierce operation of public order, in the context of terrorist attacks. This episode would serve as an example of the French wars against insurgence. Moreover, the principle of revolutionary war would eventually become useful later in the fight against communism and terrorism, and was particularly used in the Latin American anti-communist dictatorships (Argentina and Chile), during the Vietnam War (1954-1975), under the dictatorships of António de Oliveira Salazar (politician, 1889-1970) in Portugal, but also by the United States in Afghanistan and Iraq.

The principle of revolutionary war urged Western nations to develop a military theory that was able to systematically counter the guerrilla practices conducted during the fight for liberation. France played an essential role in the understanding and dissemination of this throughout the West, which is why France speaks of the end of the Algerian war as a doctrine of revolutionary war. It is based on various fundamental principles related to psychological action, such as the creation of an inner common enemy, the use of fear as a means of control, the systematic practice of torture and disappearances. Charles Lacheroy greatly contributed to its development and dissemination. In 1927, this colonial officer began his career in Syria, then under French administration, where he was confronted for the first time by the guerrillas. Assigned to Mali in 1946, he was in charge of quelling the African rebellions led by Félix Houphouët-Boigny (Ivorian statesman, 1905-1993). However, it was mainly during the war in Indochina that he developed a doctrine of revolutionary war by observing the effectiveness of the Vietnamese fighters against his own troops. Although less equipped and less trained, he noted that an army of peasants was able to triumph over a professional army. To complete his theory, he highlighted the importance of controlling the civilian population – which he called the principle of parallel hierarchies – in *The Little Red Book* by Mao Tse-tung (Chinese statesman, 1893-1976) and also studied the work of Sergei Chakhotin (Russian-born German biologist and sociologist, 1883-1973), *The rape of the masses; the psychology of totalitarian political propaganda*. At the Battle of Algiers, Charles Lacheroy would have the opportunity to put his theory into practice through the invention of the 5th office, whose mission was to establish sorting centers to detach prisoners from their joining of the FLN and to roam the desert to rally villagers to support the French cause.

The type of combat that took place during the Battle of Algiers differed radically from the war carried out previously by Westerners. The basis of this strategy dates back to the work entitled *The Art of War* by Sun Tzu (Chinese general, c. 8th century B.C.), which still serves as a reference today. The Chinese general, whose existence has never actually been confirmed, developed his strategy, which was to weaken the resistance of the enemy by affecting the morale of the troops in a non-violent manner. The art of surprise and deception were thus used in war. These methods, which relied in part on propaganda prepared behind the front, allowed for the mobilization of the civilian population. In the revolutionary war, guerrilla practices were added to this psychological manipulation, most often used by non-professional fighters driven by the ideal of independence.

During the Battle of Algiers, this urban guerrilla warfare opposed Algerian nationalists, whose main terrorist action was to place bombs in wealthy European quarters of Algiers. They also ensured the maintenance of security within their networks by threatening anyone who denounced them with death. The various networks that structured these methods were extremely complex and were based on the majority of the Muslim population being subservient to the FLN. However, other Algerian nationalist movements (NAM, Algerian Communist Party, etc.) and French Algerian movements (French Communist Party) would join forces.

The FLN exerted relentless control over the population through the system of parallel hierarchies.

Facing the FLN were the paratrooper commandos of the French army, working in collaboration with the police and gendarmerie, with the main mission of destroying these skilled terrorist networks and regaining the trust of their opponents. Their major field of action was in the kasbah of Algiers, the Muslim Quarter, which was characterized by its poverty and a very dense population of 70 000 individuals gathered in a small space. It was in this crowded space that leaders and weapons were hidden. The key to success was therefore based entirely on information. It was thus necessary to carry out the important job of meticulously deconstructing each link of the different networks, in order to get their hands on the weapons and arrest the leaders. To do this, the French troops used the technique of grid lines, the government database, infiltration of the networks and torture.

THE START OF HOSTILITIES

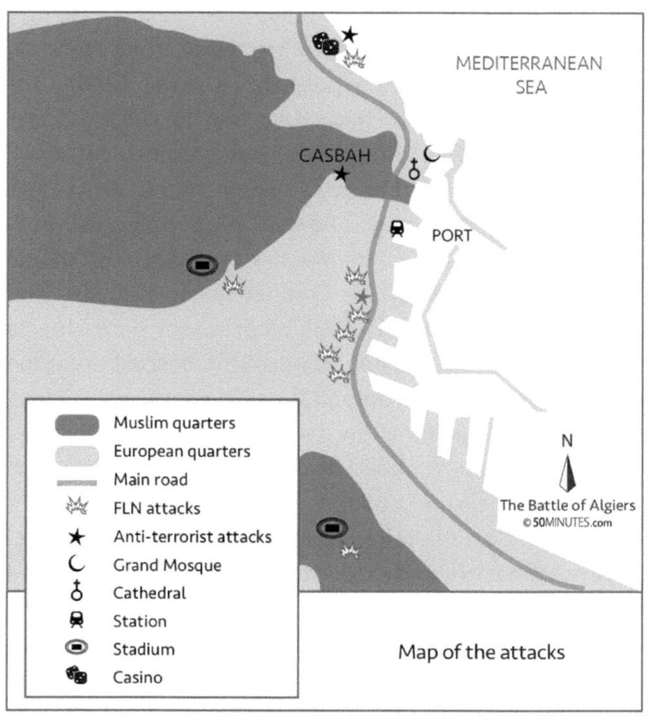

Map of the attacks

In the beginning of January, the French authorities learned that a general strike was being organized by the nationalists and was scheduled for 28 January. Considered to be an affront, this provided the French with proof that the true leader of the FLN was in Algiers. Gradually, tensions grew and a series of attacks were committed in the heart of the city.

Faced with the rising violence, the governor of Algeria, Robert Lacoste, granted full powers to General Jacques Massu on 7 January 1957. Therefore, Massu had access to everything he needed to expose the terrorist network of Algiers and dismantle it. Thus, he entered the city that same day at the head of a staff of 8 000 highly trained paratroopers, still under the influence of their victory of a few days earlier over the troops of Colonel Gamal Abdel Nasser in the Suez Canal crisis. Jacques Massu was assisted by Colonel Marcel Bigeard (1916-2010), Colonel Roger Trinquier and Colonel Yves Godard (1911-1975), all of whom were experts in revolutionary warfare methods. This descent into the kasbah aimed to deter potential participants in the strike that was scheduled for a few days later. To do this, the area was completely surrounded by barbed wire and systematic searches were carried out to the find the 1 500 members of the National Liberation Army who were hidden there. However, the entry of the paratroopers into the city caused a wave of deadly attacks.

In order to obtain the necessary information to identify suspects and carry out their arrests, each block of houses was patrolled by urban militia. To carry out their mission, the soldiers often worked at night and searched homes without warning, according to a very fast process, in which soldiers, police and military intelligence worked together. Thousands of people were monitored daily and hundreds were reported as suspicious individuals. These people were arrested and taken to a detention center. Meanwhile, thousands of individuals were interviewed by the army in secret locations. Thanks to the urban protection system set up by Colonel Roger Trinquier, the French soldiers managed to track down and arrest Mohamed Larbi Ben M'hidi, one of the nine historic leaders of the FLN and the brains behind the operations in the autonomous zone of Algiers, on 23 February 1957. The latter was captured, interrogated and executed by the firing squad of commander Paul Aussaresses. Also threatened, the coordination and implementation committee fled to Tunisia from Algiers, leaving Yacef Saâdi alone to direct the terrorist operations.

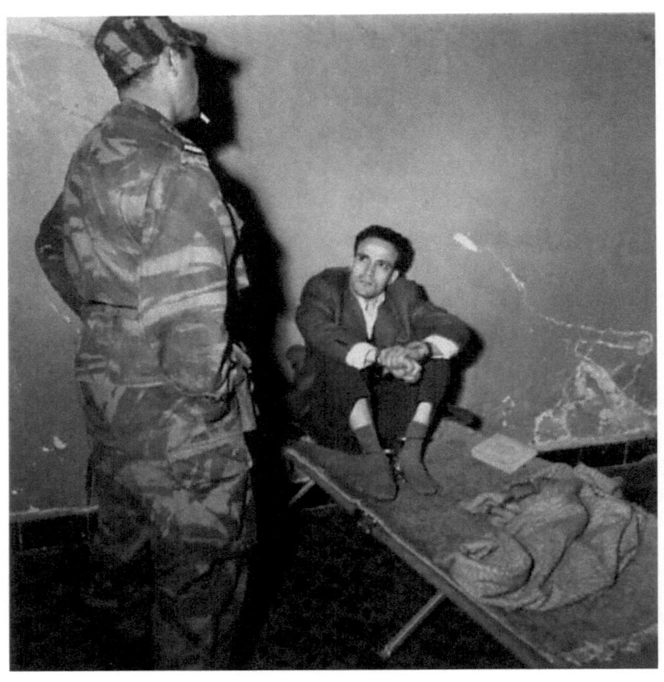

Arrest of Mohamed Larbi Ben M'hidi.

The situation settled down as attacks declined: attacks decreased from 112 in January to 29 in March 1957. However, Yacef Saâdi was determined to continue operations, assisted in his efforts by a series of committees that allowed for the organization of the attacks, propaganda and the spreading of the news overseas. He also had a drafting committee in charge of gathering information on torture, a committee of justice and a social welfare committee. By the summer of 1957, between 1 500 and 5 000 individuals had gravitated around the head of the autonomous zone of Algiers.

New actions were carried out and the attacks resumed in a very brutal manner, particularly with the attack on the Corniche casino on 3 June, resulting in the deaths of 8 people and leaving 81 wounded. Yet, as early as July, the number of members of the National Liberation Front of the autonomous Algiers zone decreased sharply. Meanwhile, the French methods became more bureaucratized, under the influence of Colonel Yves Goddard and Colonel Roger Trinquier. To facilitate the civil and military collaboration, information centers were created to try and indentify the ringleaders and neutralize them. Furthermore, a propaganda service was set up to organize the mass participation of the population in the project of Franco-Algerian integration.

INTERROGATIONS, TORTURE AND DISAPPEARANCES

During the Battle of Algiers, French soldiers used torture to dismantle the FLN. Anyone suspected of acquaintance with the front was arrested, interrogated and was likely to have provided information for fear of being tortured. The suspects were arrested in their homes, often at night, and were put under house arrest in camps. The most frequent torture method used by the French military was the "gégène", which involved inflicting electric shocks on parts of the body, waterboarding, or force-feeding through a funnel. Through this act, the French not only wanted to gain information quickly, but also frighten to population to mobilize them in their project.

During the summer of 1957, the second battle of Algiers began. Torture and propaganda campaigns intensified in the capital. The situation was therefore critical for the autonomous zone, as the number of activists had drastically decreased. With the information they collected, the French army was able to dismantle the area and follow the traces of the leaders of the Algerian Nationalist Party. The battle officially came to an end with the arrest of Yacef Saâdi on 24 September and his accomplice, Ali La Pointe (real name Ali Ammar, 1930-1957) on 8 October.

REPERCUSSIONS OF THE BATTLE

THE TRUE NATURE OF THE BATTLE

The term "battle" was used to describe the events that occurred in Algiers shortly after the entry of General Jacques Massu's troops. However, thereafter, the major players of repression, such as Colonel Marcel Bigeard, would admit to it being more of a police operation. It is therefore difficult to categorize the Battle of Algiers using a classical definition of war practice, even if the operations were indeed orchestrated by military men. In fact, the practices performed during this episode did not correspond to those of a conventional war. Thus, General Jacques Massu received police powers early on in the conflict, in order to pursue his aim of arresting the members of the FLN.

Moreover, the conflict was between nationalists, who carried out bomb attacks, and an alliance of the military and the police, who were responsible for neutralizing them. Both sides resorted to illegal practices, in violation of the laws of war and of French laws. Nevertheless, the death toll was lower than that of a traditional battle. It is estimated today that the attacks by the FLN during the nine-month-long conflict killed fewer than 400 people on the French side and between 1 000 and 3 000 on the Algerian side, which is only logical, as the actions led during the Battle of Algiers were mainly intended to terrify the populations. Recognizing this, it would be more accurate to speak primarily of a psychological battle, even if it is likely that, given the excesses of the French troops and the complaints of the public, the authorities sought to justify the violence and repression by exaggerating the warlike nature of the combat.

A HEAVILY CRITICIZED BATTLE

The escalation of violence, resulting from the terrorist attacks on the one side and the use of torture on the other, radicalized both sides, annihilating any hope of reconciliation.

Following the event, the French army faced strong protest campaigns, both abroad and in France, because of the means they used. During the battle, underground newspapers revealing the facts were distributed in France and, gradually, the officers also spoke out to denounce the atrocities that occurred in Algiers. Some resigned, such as General Jacques Pâris de la Bollardière. From then on, solidarity networks in Europe and French intellectuals took action to help the FLN. All of this forced France to relax its policy towards the nationalists, who took the opportunity to introduce the Algerian Republic.

However, this lessening of authority raised the ire of extremists from Algeria, which triggered major riots, coming close to insurgency. To fix the situation, the French people appealed to Charles de Gaulle who had received full power.

Everyone was convinced that he would find a compromise in Algeria and maintain the colony. But, on 4th June 1958, Charles de Gaulle held his famous speech in Algiers before an audience of ultras and Muslims and stated that he had understood them. Although the ultras were confident that the General would reinstate an authoritarian regime in

Algeria, his speech was immediately followed by measures establishing equal rights between French and Algerians. Nevertheless, an insurgency led by the ultras erupted, causing a general coup in April 1961, but the coup was not supported by the soldiers of the division, who provoked its failure. Under international pressure, de Gaulle finally granted independence to Algeria through the Evian agreements in March 1962.

THE BATTLE OF ALGIERS: A FRENCH VICTORY?

The Battle of Algiers thus ended in September 1957. Although the French were able to stop the attacks for a while and dismantle the FLN networks, the nationalists recovered the legitimacy of their struggle by rallying global public opinion to their cause. Indeed, international pressure would eventually convince France of the impossibility of its fight, despite strong protests from the ranks of conservatives.

The independence gained by Algeria in 1962 was actually the culmination of a process that began with the Battle of Algiers. Much more than a victory for France, this episode marked the beginning of the end of colonial rule, which the more nostalgic would eventually defend thereafter in the ranks of the extreme rights political parties in France. Independence was the beginning of a long and extremely complex task of building a national identity, which has since caused more violence and score-setting and still reminds of the wounds inflicted by colonization even today.

SUMMARY

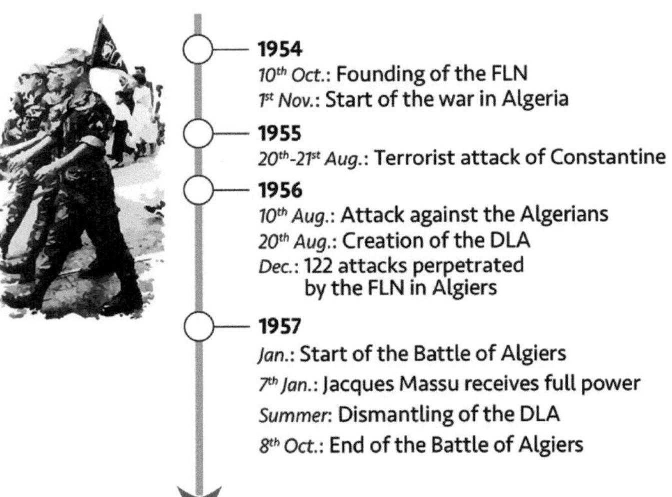

1954
10th Oct.: Founding of the FLN
1st Nov.: Start of the war in Algeria

1955
20th-21st Aug.: Terrorist attack of Constantine

1956
10th Aug.: Attack against the Algerians
20th Aug.: Creation of the DLA
Dec.: 122 attacks perpetrated
by the FLN in Algiers

1957
Jan.: Start of the Battle of Algiers
7th Jan.: Jacques Massu receives full power
Summer: Dismantling of the DLA
8th Oct.: End of the Battle of Algiers

- Algeria first became a French colony in 1830. The French population, who lost a lot of prestige and political and economic power at the end of the Great War, wanted to keep the colony despite the process of decolonization that began in 1918.

- In 1945, while the population hoped to gain independence following the Algerian commitment during the Second World War, the massacre of Sétif took place.

- On 7 May 1954, France was defeated by the troops of Ho Chi Minh at Dien Bien Phu. This insult resulted in a push to preserve what remained of France's colonial empire.

- The FLN, a nationalist Algerian independence movement, was created in October 1954. Its action was clearly directed towards an armed struggle against its occupier.

- On 1 November 1954, the FLN orchestrated a popular uprising, starting the Algerian War that would see them fight against the French armed forces.
- In August 1955, the massacre of Constantine took place, perpetrated by the FLN. In response, France sent an armed contingent to Algeria.
- In early 1956, Guy Mollet granted full power to Governor Robert Lacoste.
- In August, the French radicals committed an attack in Thebes street in the heart of the Muslim quarter.
- At the Soummam conference, the FLN created the autonomous zone of Algiers in order to take power in the capital. From August to December 1956, the number of attacks soared. Mohamed Larbi Ben M'hidi and Yacef Saâdi were responsible for organizing the capital.
- On 8 January 1957, Jacques Massu entered the kasbah of Algiers with his men, marking the beginning of the Battle of Algiers.
- The French practiced anti-insurgency warfare to dismantle the networks of the FLN.
- On 23 February 1957, Mohamed Larbi Ben M'hidi, the chief of the military zone of Algiers, was arrested, tortured and executed by the firing squad of commander Paul Aussaresses.
- On 24 September, Yacef Saâdi was arrested and imprisoned. This episode marked the end of the Battle of Algiers.

We want to hear from you!
Leave a comment on your online library
and share your favourite books on social media!

FIND OUT MORE

BIBLIOGRAPHY

- Alleg, H. (2006) *The Question*. Trans. Calder, D. Nebraska: Bison Books.
- Branche, R. (2001) *La torture et l'armée pendant la guerre d'Algérie. 1954-1962*. Paris: Gallimard.
- Connelly, M. (2002) *L'arme secrète du FLN. Comment de Gaulle a perdu la guerre d'Algérie*. Paris: Payot.
- Delmas, C. (1959) *La guerre révolutionnaire*. Paris: Presses Universitaires de France.
- Fanon, F. (2001) *The Wretched of the Earth*. Trans. Farrington, C. London: Penguin.
- Hobsbawm, E. (1995) *Age of Extremes: The Short Twentieth Century 1914-1991*. London: Abacus.
- Jauffret, J.-C. (2000) *Soldats en Algérie, 1954-1962. Expériences contrastées des hommes du contingent*. Paris: Autrement.
- Jauffret, J.-C. and Vaisse, M. (2001) *Militaires et guérilla dans la guerre d'Algérie*. Brussels: Complexe.
- Meynier, G. (2002) *Histoire du FLN (1954-1962)*. Paris: Fayard.
- Milza, P. (1996) *Les relations internationales de 1871 à 1914*. Paris: Armand Colin.
- Pellissier, P. (1995) *La bataille d'Alger*. Paris: Perrin.
- Peries, G. and Servenay, D. (2007) *Une guerre noire. Enquête sur les origines du génocide rwandais (1959-1994)*. Paris: La Découverte.
- Peyroulou, J.-P. (2009) *Guelma, 1945. Une subversion française dans l'Algérie coloniale*. Paris: La Découverte.

- Rigouste, M. (2009) *L'ennemi intérieur. La généalogie coloniale et militaire de l'ordre sécuritaire dans la France contemporaine*. Paris: La Découverte.
- Roben, M.-M. (2008) *Escadrons de la mort, l'école française*. Paris: La Découverte.
- Stora, B. (2004) *Histoire de la guerre d'Algérie (1954-1962)*. Paris: La Découverte.
- Trinquier, R. (2000) *Modern Warfare: A French View of Counterinsurgency*. Trans. Lee, D. Westport, Connecticut: Praeger Security International.

ADDITIONAL SOURCES

- Alexander, M.S. and Keiger, J.F.V. (eds.) (2002) *France and the Algerian War, 1954-1962: Strategy, Operations and Diplomacy*. London: Frank Cass Publishers.
- Evans, M. (2013) *Algeria: France's Undeclared War*. Oxford: Oxford University Press.
- Horne, A. (2006) *A Savage War of Peace: Algeria 1954-1962*. New York: NYRB Classics.
- Shepard, T. (2008) *The Invention of Decolonization: The Algerian War and the Remaking of France*. New York: Cornell University Press.

ICONOGRAPHIC SOURCES

- Parade of the 10th parachute division of general Massu, summer 1957. Royalty-free reproduction picture
- Dismantling of the "Bomb" network in June 1957. Royalty-free reproduction picture.
- Arrest of Mohamed Larbi Ben M'hidi. © Leader during

the Algerian war of independence.